Get That Grant!
The Quick-Start Guide to
Successful Proposals

Second Edition

Gail R. Shapiro, Ed.M.
and
Carla C. Cataldo, M.P.P.

Acknowledgements

Get That Grant! The Quick-Start Guide to Successful Proposals, Second Edition first was published in 2006, under the title *Introduction to Grant Proposal Writing: A Self-Study Guide.* This edition, updated and revised to reflect recent trends in proposal writing, incorporates many comments and suggestions from our readers. We are grateful for this input. We are especially grateful to Russ Johnson for his excellent peer review of the manuscript.

We also wish to thank our clients, colleagues, students, and workshop participants for the opportunity to continue to learn and improve our skills throughout the years; as well as our families for their support.

With the exception of Womankind's Financial Literacy Project and the national organizations cited with attribution, all projects, programs, and examples described herein are fictional.

Table of Contents

Forward

Whether you are a writer who is looking to expand your skills, a newcomer to the development field, or a non-profit Executive Director who needs to brush up on proposal writing techniques, this *Guide* is for you.

The eight lessons will help you learn both how to write a compelling, comprehensive grant proposal, and to think like a successful proposal writer. Each lesson presents information about the mechanics of proposal writing as well as questions posed to sharpen your thought process. Finally, in many lessons, we challenge you to stop, take pen (or keyboard) in hand, and complete an exercise. By completing all the exercises, you will walk through the process of creating a complete proposal.

In order to get the maximum benefit from this *Guide*, you will need:

- Employment at or access to a non-profit organization (NPO), and
- A purpose for which funding is needed, such as a project, a program, equipment, or a building.

If you do not have these, you can invent a project and/or organization for learning purposes or you can use a department of your local municipality (e.g. Senior Center or Parks & Recreation Department).

What you will learn

By using *The Quick-Start Guide to Successful Proposals*, you will learn how to:

- Turn your good idea or project into a marketable plan
- Clearly organize your project and create measurable objectives
- Identify and produce elements common to most successful proposals
- Create a realistic budget
- Think about customizing your proposal to meet funder guidelines
- Figure out where to begin and how to refine your funder research
- Begin to approach funders, and

- Plan for follow-up once the grant is submitted.

Proceed to **Lesson One**.

Lesson One: Get Started

How does proposal writing fit into the big picture of fundraising?

Grant proposal writing is just one component of an organization's overall fundraising plan. "Fundraising" is the term often used by those outside the field for development. "Development" is the identification, cultivation, solicitation, and stewardship of prospective funders in order to secure monetary or in-kind gifts from individuals, as well as from corporations, foundations, and the government, in support of an institution and its programs.

Development is only one component of a comprehensive plan to support and promote an organization. Sometimes referred to as "Institutional Advancement," this plan interweaves many functions, including, but not limited to: strategic planning, public relations, publications, marketing, special events, corporate and foundation relations, and grants management. Institutional Advancement also weaves together many individual and departmental participants, including: members, constituents, clients, the Board of Trustees, the Board President, senior staff, support staff, committees, the Development Office, the Business Office, and any external fundraising counsel or advisors.

Development is One Component of Institutional Advancement

All the components are, or should be, driven by the mission of the organization, its goals, and the objectives designed to meet those goals. The mission, goals, and objectives (sometimes also called "strategies" or "action steps") are the foundation of the organization's strategic plan, which is developed by the Board of Directors, often with input from senior staff, consultants, and sometimes from other constituents.

Grants are but one of the revenue components of a well-constructed Strategic Plan for Development. As you can see by the following diagram, there are numerous components.

Revenue Components

The challenges

Like other professions, development has its own rules and best practices, created throughout the years. As true today as when he said it more than forty years ago, according to fundraising guru Harold J. Seymour: "Good laws and principles of organized fundraising are a priceless gift of the long years … ignored or trifled with at your peril." (*Designs for Fundraising: Principles, Patterns, Techniques*. New York: McGraw-Hill, 1966).

Unfortunately, many agencies and Board members incorrectly think that finding grant money is a panacea – the solution to all their funding needs and fiscal woes. Don't make the mistake of believing that seeking grants is a substitute for a comprehensive strategic plan and development plan.

Sources of charitable contributions

So that you do not waste time or money, know that seeking grants is *not* the best or the fastest solution to an organization's fiscal challenges or even basic needs. In fact, 90% of the revenue an organization will raise will come from other sources, and typically just 10% will come from grants.

In 2008, about 82% of all charitable gifts in the United States were made by individuals, both during their lifetime (75%) and through bequests (7%). Corporations made about 5% of gifts, and foundations about 13% (*Giving USA 2009*, Giving USA Foundation ™). Although the total amount of giving was down in 2008, these percentages have remained remarkably consistent during the fifty or so years that they have been tracked, and are not expected to change significantly in the foreseeable future.

During the lessons that follow, we will not elaborate on how to secure gifts from individuals, nor will we cover major gifts, special events, or annual funds, although grant proposal writing is directly related to all these other functions of development.

What can grant funds be used for?

Funders normally earmark their grants for one or more of the following:

- PROJECTS and PROGRAMS: Direct services or research.
- CAPITAL needs: Buildings, land, and major equipment.
- OPERATIONS: The day-to-day costs of running the organization, including salaries, rents, utilities, and other regular expenses.
- ENDOWMENT: Funds invested for future use by the organization. Normally all but a small percentage of the capital is left untouched, and only the interest is drawn upon.

- EMERGENCIES: An occurrence outside the normal operations of the organization, which could not have been foreseen, and which is expected to be a one-time or temporary situation.

- PASS-THROUGH GRANTS: Scholarships or other funds for which individuals can apply directly, or funds provided to an organization which then are distributed to its own students or clients.

- CAPACITY BUILDING: Funds used to help an organization build its ability to operate more efficiently or effectively, for example, to upgrade computers or to hire a marketing or fundraising consultant.

- SPONSORSHIPS: Corporate or foundation funds dedicated to a single event.

- MATCHING FUNDS: A grant made specifically to match other funds obtained for any of the purposes above.

To find the best possible match for your needs, look at prospective funders' giving in terms of the above categories, plus these:

- DIRECT SERVICES: Some funders provide support only for direct services to people or animals.

- PILOT PROGRAMS AND MODEL INITIATIVES: Many funders seek to increase their impact by funding the development of a model program which may be able to be replicated elsewhere.

- TYPE OF AGENCY: Funders often have a particular area of interest, such as human services, education, advocacy, research, arts, or other type of organization.

- GEOGRAPHIC LOCATION: Most corporate and many other foundations fund only in their areas of operation and/or headquarters.

- SOURCE(S) OF OTHER FUNDING: Some funders will not support organizations already receiving funds from other established sources, such as the United Way. Others will fund your organization only if they know that it already has a broad base of support.

- START-UP (SEED) VERSUS ESTABLISHED: Some funders will support only brand-new organizations or those with a very small annual operating budget, while others will not consider a proposal until the applicant NPO is at least three years old, with a strong record of success.

- POPULATION SERVED: Funders often cite populations of interest, such as immigrants, the disabled, veterans, girls and women, homeless, children, symphony-goers, or residents of a particular city or county.
- RECENCY OR FREQUENCY: Some funders prefer to grant to familiar, previously-funded organizations, while others allow you to apply only once every two or three years.

Do you really want a grant?

Before you spend the many hours and do all the work it takes to produce a grant proposal, it is a good idea to ask yourself if you even need a grant. Might there be other ways to implement your idea? How has your organization accomplished things and started new projects so far? Some organizations with which we work:

- Use volunteers, interns, or students who will work for academic credit;
- Share part-time employees, known as "Circuit Riders," with other non-profit organizations;
- Charge a fee for their services or ask for a donation for their services;
- Barter with another non-profit for complementary services; or,
- Drop an existing time-consuming or inefficient service, in order to free up resources for new projects.

All grants received require some amount of paperwork, including reporting to the funder quarterly or at the end of the funding period. Some funders want to make site visits, usually but not always announced, for which your organization must prepare. There may be specific accounting requirements, which necessitate changes in your established accounting procedures. How much of your Executive Director's or management staff's time will be spent on overseeing the program or project if it is funded? What about your financial staff? Is the amount of the grant worth the investment of your time and energy?

The adult education program in a small Midwestern town was eligible for a $3000 grant from a national foundation to study the efficacy of the classes it offers at the local high school. When the Director of the program received and reviewed the grant guidelines, she noted the semi-annual reporting requirements for grant recipients, which, as expected, *included a narrative report on the progress of the research, any deviations from the proposed timeline, and a financial report on grant expenditures.*

However, she was dismayed to find that the foundation required a separate description for "each task or logical segment of work on which effort was expended" during the grant period. This description was to include "relevant data and detailed graphs sufficient to explain the significant results achieved and any preliminary conclusions resulting from the analysis and scientific evaluation of data," a "description of current technical or substantive performance," as well as "a detailed description of difficulties encountered, with plans to address them in the future."

The Director quickly realized that the relatively small size of the grant would not even match the amount needed to compensate her over-worked staff for their time to prepare the report. She declined to apply.

For this grant program or idea, will your organization need additional supplies or equipment? Will you need more space in order to implement this idea, and if so, where will you get it? In other words, being able to obtain and manage a grant requires organizational capacity. Most funders will not provide grant funds for the organizational staffing and systems to manage a grant – your organization will have to be able to handle the internal systems to effectively utilize and account for grant funds. The cost will have to be borne by the organization's existing operating funds, as a match to the grant dollars.

Before you begin to write

Once you have received the Board of Directors' or Executive Director's blessing to proceed with the proposal, before you begin to write it is vital to be sure that your organization:

- Has incorporated as a non-profit organization, and has applied for and been granted 501(c)(3) status by the Internal Revenue Service. Municipal governments are non-profits by definition and do not need an IRS determination. Most religious organizations also are non-profits, but should obtain a letter of determination in case the funder requests or requires it.

If your organization does not yet have such status, it will need to find a fiscal sponsor who does. A fiscal sponsor, also called a "fiduciary agent," is another non-profit organization which agrees to apply for and administer grant funds on behalf of a charitable program or project not yet incorporated and/or recognized by the Internal Revenue Service. The fiscal sponsor usually oversees the accounting, reporting and other administration on behalf of your organization. Normally, the fiscal sponsor will retain a small fee or percentage of the funds received (about 5% is typical) for administration and oversight of your grant. This amount will be included in the budget you submit to the funder.

- Is financially stable, with a clear mission and goals, and a good plan to implement those goals. Does it have, or is it prepared to hire, a staff with the credentials and experience necessary to carry out its work? In addition, the organization and its work must fill a community need, and it should have active support from community members.

- Can show, if it is a brand new non-profit, that it has some initial capital, or at least a development plan to raise money. Some NPOs accomplish this by having members of the Board of Directors loan some start-up funds to get the organization off the ground. Others seek outright donations of seed money from Board members or other supporters.

- Puts its fiscal house in order. This means making sure that the books are up-to-date, the latest IRS Form 990 return is filed, and that it has met any state requirements for filing, such as registration with the state's Bureau of Charities and/or the Attorney General's office. If the agency has revenues greater than $200,000 annually and has not had an audit or financial review for the last fiscal year within ninety days of the books closing, that is a warning sign to prospective funders and the public about its fiscal management capacity. The organization also needs to have a solid financial manager or team in place. Check to see that your organization's most recent IRS Form 990 has been posted on Guidestar.org, since foundations and donors are likely to look there.

- Gains support, or at least cooperation, from all involved.

- Budgets enough time to do a thorough job. How long does it take to write a good proposal? While it can vary greatly depending on the nature and complexity of the project, the experience of the writer, and the specific requirements of the funder, a good rule-of-thumb for the new grant proposal writer is to allow at least 40 hours to prepare a simple proposal for a corporation or foundation. Double that figure for more complicated projects or for government proposals. Halve that time if you are experienced.

- Allows ample time for the finished proposal to be proofread and produced. If your proposal will require letters of support, detailed financial information, or other supporting documents, which may not be at your fingertips, you may need an extra week or more. Plan ahead! Most grant proposal writing consultants or NPO development officers have had the experience of the eager call about a great grant opportunity that is due in a day or two, with the anxious caller asking, "Can you help us?" or, "Can we do it?" Most of the time, the correct answer is "no." For most NPOs, dropping everything to meet a tight deadline probably will not result in a successful proposal.

- Obtains formal consent from partners or collaborators, if any are involved in the program or project. Be sure to obtain a letter from each partner's Executive Director and/or Board Secretary. Some foundations have a "consortium agreement form," when a collaboration is involved, while others may require a formal Board resolution from each participating organization.

- Has or can build the capacity to fulfill all grant commitments. Does the organization have the support of the program staff who will implement the project and manage the finances? Otherwise when the grant is received, it will be problematic for the organization. If staff does not fulfill the grant requirements and carry out the program on time and on budget, the funder is likely to deny future support and possibly even demand that funds be returned.

- Has developed a realistic strategic plan for fundraising, so that expected grant revenues will meet about ten percent of the organization's needed income. One exception to this rule is in the case of a start-up organization. Grants may constitute a much larger initial percentage of the budget, as the new organization starts to build a donor base of individuals. Remember: by definition, "development" takes time! Also, every member of the Board of Directors should have made his or her own financial gift, in addition to whatever volunteer time he or she may be giving. If those closest and most committed to the goals of the organization are not supporting it, why should anyone else?

- Understands that not every grant proposal will be funded. For example, assuming that your organization has an excellent, well-developed project that matches the criteria of the prospective funder, and assuming that you follow all the steps in this *Guide*, it might reasonably expect to get approximately 10-25% of the grant money for which it applies. Although this number may sound low, remember that your NPO will be competing with many other worthwhile projects and organizations for the same funds. It is important that the Board, staff, and you, yourself have realistic expectations.

▶ **Exercise:**

Consider whether or not you actually need a grant. How else might you raise money for your program or project other than by applying for grants? Identify and list at least two other possible options. You can use these options now, in addition to a grant, or later, in case your first tries at proposal writing do not succeed.

Once all of these steps are in place, proceed to **Lesson Two.**

Lesson Two: Find the Best Potential Funders

Writing a proposal can begin in one of two ways: you develop a fundable idea and seek out and approach appropriate funders, or you can respond to a Request for Proposals (RFP), also known as a Request for Responses (RFR). RFPs often are generated by the government, and also sometimes by larger foundations.

If you start with your own idea, here is what the process may look like:

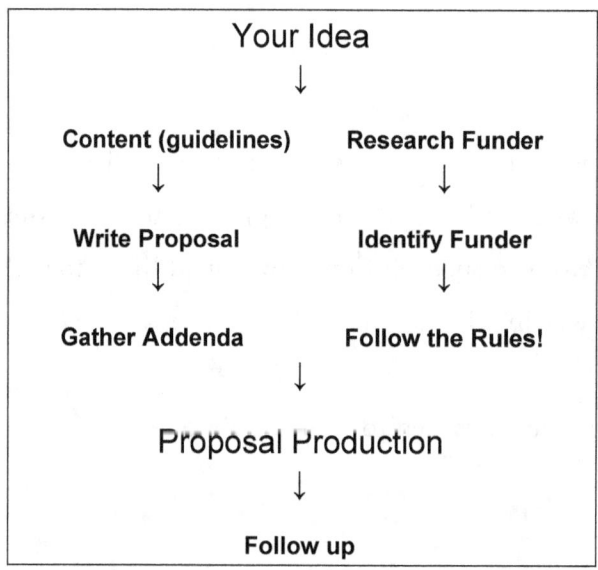

In other words, starting with your good idea, you will begin to develop the content of the proposal at the same time you begin to look for one or more funders. You need to do these two things simultaneously. As mentioned, some funders focus on projects, some on operations, some on buildings or equipment, and so on. The actual content of your proposal will be informed by the funders you choose and vice versa.

If you are responding to an RFP, you would:

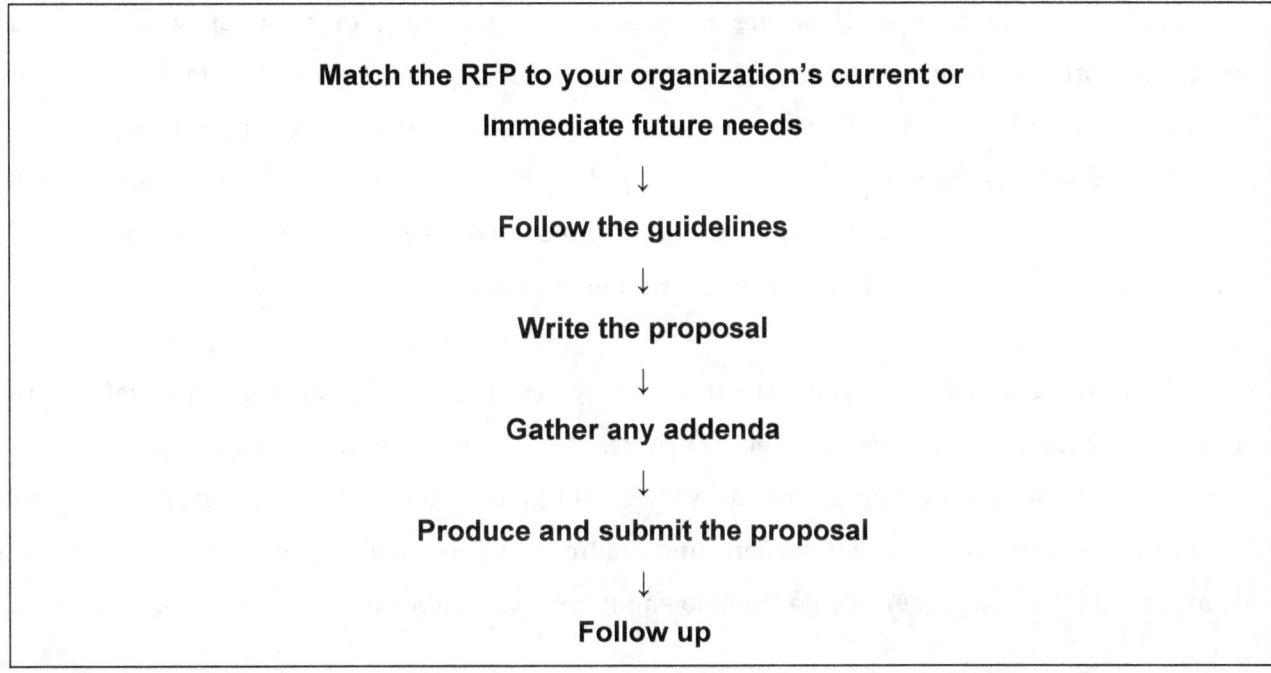

Match the RFP to your organization's current or

Immediate future needs

↓

Follow the guidelines

↓

Write the proposal

↓

Gather any addenda

↓

Produce and submit the proposal

↓

Follow up

It is very important to read the RFP (or guidelines) carefully and assess them realistically. Is the RFP a good match, a fair match, or a poor match with your organizational mission and programming? The more one has to modify a program or mission to make it fit the RFP, the less likely it is that it is a good match, and the less likely it is to get funded.

Some funders prefer that you send a short Letter of Inquiry, normally one to three pages in length, describing your proposed project or program. If your idea interests the funder, you will be invited to submit a full proposal. This saves time and effort, both for the funder and for the NPO.

How will you find one or more appropriate funding possibilities?

Sources of foundation funding

In addition to government grants, other sources of funding include the various types of foundations: independent, community, and corporate.

Independent (or Private) Foundations can be family foundations, special purpose foundations, or multipurpose foundations. Family foundations are established by individuals or families with accumulated wealth, and can be set up with broad or narrow guidelines, according to the wishes of the founders. Some have staff or are managed by a law firm or trust officers at a financial institution; others are managed by a Board of Directors, often comprised of family members and friends. The smaller the foundation, the less likely it is to have any staff, or to have a website, published guidelines, annual reports, or other publications. Many larger foundations publish their guidelines on their website; others do not. If you cannot find a small foundation's guidelines, you can request them via a very brief letter or note, or an email message.

A special purpose foundation limits its grantmaking activity to one or more specific fields of interest or limits giving to a few pre-selected charities. For example, within this category are the 145 women's funds, which fund programs for women and girls in their specific geographic communities. In contrast, a multi-purpose foundation funds many different fields of interest, and often, but not always, tends to make larger grants than do small family foundations.

Community Foundations fund a specific geographic region, such as New York City (The New York Foundation and The New York Community Trust), a metropolitan area (The Minneapolis Foundation), or a county (Dade Community Foundation). They represent the combined resources of many donors, rather than of one family or individual. Community foundations may solicit and/or accept gifts from a broad segment of the community they represent, which they then distribute to community-based groups via grants. Community foundations often are interested in capacity building. They also may provide advice and training for grant seekers.

Corporate Foundations are established by a corporation. Some have dedicated staff; some do not. They tend to be geographically sensitive, giving in locations where they have an office or plant, or in the areas from which they draw their labor pool. Or, a corporation may not have a separate foundation, but may make matching grants for the gifts their employees give to non-profits. Corporate giving often is managed by the company's public relations or community affairs office. If this is the case, it may be assumed that the company desires some recognition in return for its support.

Often, foundations will make gifts to charities they select, and *will not accept* any requests for funding at all. Make sure to check this first as you begin your research, by looking for phrases like "gives to pre-selected organizations only" or "unsolicited proposals not accepted."

For the purpose of this *Guide*, you will be responding to a government RFP or approaching a foundation, in contrast to soliciting a business. But don't neglect the marketing and advertising monies from local companies – often they have a much larger pool of dollars than does the company's foundation. A new retailer moving into your community can be a new source of funding. Be sure to ask!

In order to find these potential funders, your local grantmaking library is the first place to start. More than 380 such libraries across the country, affiliated with The Foundation Center, are called Cooperating Collections and can be found at this link: http://foundationcenter.org/collections/.

These Cooperating Collections are free funding information centers, located in libraries, community foundations, and other such sites that offer services and resources to the non-profit community. Cooperating Collections are located in all fifty states, plus the District of Columbia and Puerto Rico.

Materials include both Foundation Center and other publications useful to grant seekers, funders, and donors. Print sources normally include reference books that must be used in the Library, as well as books that circulate. Best of all, they often provide a computer work station with access to online, searchable directories of thousands of foundations and government grant programs.

To search an online directory, use key words related to your area of operation. For example, if yours is an environmental organization, you can search for "education" or "environment" or "animal welfare" or "conservation." You would search for "human services" or "underprivileged youth" or "education" if your organization provides programs for the children of the homeless. You can search for "start-up" or "capacity building" if your organization is new or needs organizational development funds. You also can search by geographic location by entering your metropolitan area, state or region of the country.

Government funding

As you learned in Lesson One, government grants typically are announced through a Request for Proposals or Responses. A good way to stay on top of the myriad of such funding opportunities is to ask your local city, state, and federal representatives if they know of funding sources available for your organization's work. Touch base with them regularly.

To increase your chance of finding a government grant, you should familiarize yourself with the following resources: www.Grants.gov, your state's web page, the US Catalog of Federal Domestic Assistance (www.cfda.gov), paid publication and subscription services specializing in federal, state and/or local grants, in addition to newsletters or bulletins from any specific professional sector associations to which you or the organization you represent may belong.

▶ **Exercises:**

1. Do one of the following to locate at least five possible funders for your project:

- If you live near one of the several regional grant maker libraries, schedule a visit. Ask if they give an introductory course on how to use the Foundation Center's Directory online, or an equivalent database service. Take the course, and familiarize yourself with the available resources.

- If you do not live near a regional library, locate a public or university library near you that has a grant research section. If you prefer to work from your home or office, you can subscribe online to The Foundation Center's online database service, which as of this writing is available starting at $19.95 for a one-month basic subscription. They have an excellent tutorial on how to use their resources. Complete the tutorial and start to explore appropriate funding sources for your project. You also can sign up to receive automatic email alerts of new RFPs on the Philanthropy News Digest web page (www.foundationcenter.org/pnd/).

- Go to your State's home web page, and search for a listing of state grants, or a service that might track them. Or go to a specific department that relates to your field, and check for available grant opportunities, service contracts available, and open RFRs.

- Go to www.Grants.gov, "Find Grant Opportunities," search for grant opportunities, and sign up for a "Grant Opportunity Email Alert" for the agency or issue area of your choice.

2. Once you have located at least five possible sources of funding for your project, read the guidelines for each carefully. Decide which one is the best possible match for your project, and use that in the exercises that follow as you develop your template proposal.

Proceed to **Lesson Three**.

Lesson Three: Develop Your Case

With at least one of the good possible funding sources that you identified in Lesson Two, you can start to write a draft of your proposal. The following questions will help you begin the grant proposal writing process. This exercise assumes that project support is sought. If you prefer, you may substitute "your agency" (if seeking operating, endowment, or capital funds) for "your project" in answering the questions.

Please be aware that the questions that follow are merely guidelines. Not all funders require the same information; not all require information at the same level of detail. Suggestions as to length also are guidelines. *Always* refer to and abide by the specific funder's instructions.

What is the purpose of your project?

What is the purpose of your proposed project? State simply and clearly, in one sentence, what it is you are trying to do.

> *Bleeker College seeks to develop, implement and evaluate a new program, Fresh Start, to facilitate the school-to-college transition and provide proactive academic and life skills support for at-risk students.*

> *Springfield Union Hospital has established a new program called "Move to Win!" to provide overweight adolescents and their parents with exercise instruction, nutritional counseling, and a support group to help promote fitness, healthy eating, self-esteem and a more positive body image.*

► **Exercise:**

Write your own proposed project description. Ask someone who is not familiar with your project to review it for clarity. Revise if necessary.

Describing the problem

What problem will this project attempt to address? In proposal writing, problems are good! The bigger the problem, the stronger the case for funds can be. But describing the problem often is the single most difficult paragraph of the proposal to write, and it may take several tries to get it right. You will need to keep refining and improving upon your answer until you have distilled down to its essence the actual problem you are trying to address.

You will not be describing the NPO's problem, such as a shortage of staff or funds; you will be describing the *community's* problem. When you think of the problem to be solved, think of what you will accomplish (solve) if you receive grant funds (i.e. the outcome). Keep in mind that funders pay for *outcomes*: your staff, equipment, and overhead are just means to that end!

If the funder gives you all the money you need, what will be the more desirable situation created by your project? This solution you are attempting to achieve often is the "outcome" in a Logic Model, a tool that many funders now require (you will learn more about Logic Models in the next lesson).

▶   **Exercise:**

Write the first draft of your problem statement. Now look at what you have written. *Why* is this a problem?

For example, if your project is to provide after-school homework support and activities for middle school children, you might have written the following as a problem statement:

> *Many of the children of Landry Middle School have only one parent, who works during the day. These pre-teens go home to an empty house for several hours each afternoon.*

Why is this a problem? It certainly is a potential problem for the child and his or her parent(s), but why is it a problem for the community? In your next try, give more background information:

The Landry Middle School district is one of the poorest in the city, and has the highest crime rate, as well as the highest arrest rate for drugs. Unsupervised youngsters in this neighborhood are exposed to opportunities to get involved with alcohol or other drugs at a rate much higher than in the Springfield metropolitan area.

Again, why is this exposure a problem?

Experimentation with alcohol and other drugs may lead to addiction and to crime to support the addiction. Unsupervised adolescents also may get involved in planned or unplanned sexual activity, which may result in pregnancy, STDs, and emotional trauma. The children in this neighborhood already are at risk for school drop-out, low grades, and a host of other problems.

Why should the funder care? This may seem like a ridiculous question – and the answer patently obvious – but remember that your proposal will be competing for dollars against many other worthy projects. You will need to convince the funder of the magnitude of the problem, and make him or her want to participate in solving it. You also need to show that you understand the field, the problems and the possible solutions. For example:

The cost of this experimentation and high-risk behavior is extremely high, both to society in terms of lost potential of its youth, to actual dollar costs for increased health and police services that it necessitates.

Having thoroughly analyzed the problem, your final problem statement will look like this:

The Landry School District has one of the highest dropout and crime rates in the city. Unsupervised children are at great risk not only for school failure, but are likely to be exposed to opportunities for illegal activities and risky behaviors. Too many Landry parents have to choose between keeping their paychecks and providing a safe, supervised environment after school, resulting in potential high costs to the community in city health and police services as well as lost potential of our youth.

▶ **Exercise:**

Write the next draft of your problem statement, and keep refining it as you go along through the rest of the steps.

Constructing the case

Next, you will construct a "case" for this problem. It will be a narrative, approximately one to five paragraphs, citing current statistics, reports, and literature in your field. In other words, why should the funder take your word that this is a problem?

Also known as a "statement of need" or "case statement," this section normally requires some research. As you describe the problem and its background, how will you build a strong, convincing case? You can draw upon local, state and national statistics, government planning documents, information from professional publications and associations, and even from your own NPO's clients.

Be sure that your data are accurate, current, and that you do not generalize – for example, by applying national statistics to your community if they do not apply. Use logic, not overblown emotion, to build your case. Let the facts speak for themselves. Do not make the case sound so dire that no amount of funding can help! Present a realistic, solvable problem, so you can show how you are going to try to address it.

▶ **Exercise:**

Write a draft of your case statement. Then compare it with the following examples.

Sample case statement: Community women's center

Why do women need to know about their finances?

Reluctance to think about or take responsibility for their own financial well-being may lead to bad financial decisions, lost opportunities, or being taken advantage of at work, at home, or during a divorce or other legal action. Historically, women have received little societal support for, or training in, managing money. According to the US Dept. of

Labor, fully 90% of women currently supported by someone else – parents, partner, or the government – will at some point be handling finances on their own. As our students report, those currently managing their own or their family's finances certainly could use more education and encouragement.

As hundreds of women here in the Boston area know all too well, economic dependence equals vulnerability. No woman should be stuck in a bad or abusive relationship because she has no other viable option for herself and her children.

The problems of gender-based inequity are enormous, and affect women of all backgrounds and income levels. Because so many women drop in and out of the workforce to raise families or care for aging parents, they often are not adequately protected by traditional pension plans or even by Social Security. Women working at low-paying jobs – even those working a full, forty-hour week – may not have decent childcare and adequate, affordable health care. In more affluent households, most women would find it difficult to maintain her family's economic status on her income alone.

At Womankind, we believe that every woman – no matter what her age or current situation – needs to feel confident that she can take care of herself.

Sample case statement: After-school technology club

The Landry School seeks to excite students about the impact of technology and to inspire them to pursue math, science and technology studies through its new after-school "Tech Club."

The need to rekindle young people's interest in these disciplines is crucial, as widely-publicized reports of America's "knowledge gap" indicate. The International Assessment of Educational Proficiency showed that American nine-year-olds and thirteen-year-olds scored only low-to-mid range in both math and science, relative to the fifteen nations studied. The recent mathematics survey conducted by the US Department of Education found that 95% of American high school students lacked the mathematical knowledge to succeed in college-level courses or to perform in technological jobs. Even in the highest-scoring states, only one in four eighth graders could handle simple algebra and basic geometry.

The National Educational Goals Panel reported that students, particularly female students, in the higher grades have less positive attitudes towards mathematics and science than do students in the lower grades. The National Science Foundation found that fewer students are choosing math- and science-related college majors, and that this trend is particularly significant among girls and students of color. According to the US Department of Education, "most [high] schools find fewer girls and students of color in advanced math and science [classes]."

For these reasons, the Landry Middle School, with its high population of students of color, is offering its after-school Tech Club. At this age, students are still impressionable and eager to learn. The intent is to capture students' interest before they decide – as do many girls and minorities – that they cannot succeed in mathematics, science, or technology.

The goal is to build a convincing case in just a few paragraphs, complete with federal and/or agency-based statistics. You will add background information and a description of your proposed solution to the problem as you continue this exercise.

What other solutions have been tried?

What currently is being done to address this problem? Again, a literature review should yield other institutions or groups seeking similar ends. Even though the funder may be in the same field of interest as your NPO, you need to convince them that you know the field, as well as the other important "players," if any. Who else is doing what you propose to do, either in your community or elsewhere in the country? Are their results good, or do their attempted solutions fall short of the desired solution? How will your project succeed where these others do not?

Sample description of the competition

The Financial Literacy Project is different from every other program of financial education for women that we have identified. Nearly all "educational" programs and seminars on money management are presented with the intent of selling financial products or services. Of those geared specifically for women, most do not address the particular needs of those in low-income brackets, or those with limited education. Only a few try to address the psychology of women and money, or women's specific economic needs.

One such program, "You and Your Money," is presented by the EFG Foundation. Specifically addressed to women older than 65, the material sounds condescending in tone, assuming that these women are widows whose high-earning husbands took care of all the money decisions, that they know nothing about finances, and that they do not want to learn ("we know this is confusing and not fun for you..."). It disregards the fact that not all women in this age bracket once were married, or are ignorant about or uncomfortable with money.

Another program, developed by MNO Corporation for working mothers, assumes a much higher level of knowledge than does Womankind's program. For example, it presents a unit on how to balance a stock portfolio and information on investing in speculative ventures.

In contrast, the Financial Literacy Project is a basic course that sensitively and respectfully provides women and older girls with all levels of prior knowledge with the information and skills they need to confidently manage their finances, and prepares them for a more secure economic future.

Perhaps your project will replicate a program elsewhere in the country or your state. If that is the case, you can briefly name and describe the program and its outcomes. Then you will tell why it will be beneficial to bring it to your community, and why yours is the organization to do so.

Sample description of model replication

With the high rate of unemployment in Bleeker County, and the fact that many of our students are low-income, single mothers seeking to improve their family's economic status, a program that provides free, professional-quality clothing for job interviews is greatly needed here. After reviewing several models, we have chosen to apply for affiliate status with Dress for Success® Worldwide, a program with similar goals.

Founded in 1954, the Bleeker College Alumni Association has long been committed to supporting our community. With more than 2500 active members in seventeen regional chapters who have the interest and the capacity to carry out a similar program for our graduates, and a successful international model upon which to draw, we anticipate the ability to serve more than 500 Bleeker County women annually as they return to the workforce.

► **Exercise:**

Incorporating the answers to these questions, revise your case statement. Once you have made a strong case for your project, move on to **Lesson Four**, where you will develop your project in greater detail.

Lesson Four: Describe Your Project and Methods

This is a critical section, because a poor program design will sink your proposal. If you are developing a new project, then writing this section carefully is the most important use of your time. You will need to include *all* the details involved in creating a project from the ground up. Your project must be well thought-out, realistic, and often collaborative, among your organization's departments and sometimes with outside organizations as well. (You will learn more about collaborations in the next lesson.)

Tips for writing a good program description include:

- Explain the rationale for choosing what you are going to do and how you are going to do it (your "methods"). Are the methods based on research findings, expert opinion, anecdotal information, best practices established for your field, and/or on the agency's own experience with this or a similar program?
- State what facilities, space, and capital equipment will be available, and what will need to be obtained.
- Specify what staff will be needed and what qualifications they must have.
- Build a timeline showing various phases of activities in a linear, logical manner to move toward the desired result.
- Be specific. Do not assume the proposal reviewer knows a great deal about your project or about your NPO's field.
- Use strong verbs to create measurable objectives.

Know the terminology

As you develop your proposal, you will be asked to define your organization's mission, goals, and objectives, and often to provide detailed information on the inputs, activities, and outcomes for your project. Some organizations also have a "vision statement." It is important to be clear on what each of these terms means. However, as you read and respond to different funders' guidelines, you may find a lot of discrepancies in terminology.

We offer the following definitions to help keep you on track, especially when a specific funder does not offer a clear set of guidelines.

A **Mission Statement** is an idealistic and concise statement of why the NPO exists.

A Mission Statement expresses three elements: business, purpose, and values, though one or more of these may be implied. In other words, why does the organization exist, what is its aim, and by what principles does it operate? The mission is not measurable, nor does it tell *how* the organization is going to accomplish the mission. It should be both succinct and lofty, so that it is memorable and inspiring. For example:

> ***Womankind's Financial Literacy Project*** *helps women become financially literate and economically self-sufficient.*

> ***Bleeker College*** *seeks to advance the theory and practice of learning, and to nurture and prepare young minds for today's diverse and ever-changing world.*

> *The mission of the* ***Shangri-La Senior Service Center*** *is to improve the lives and well-being of elders in our community.*

A **Vision Statement** is the philosophy of how the NPO works
and accomplishes its mission.

The Vision Statement sometimes may include the values by which the organization operates. Here is an example:

> *Bleeker College is committed to its position as the leading institution of higher learning in Bleeker County. We believe that an educated populace is the cornerstone of a free and democratic society. We continually seek to advance the quality of students,*

facility, programs, and facilities. Bleeker College will continue to strive to make higher education affordable and accessible to our community of learners. We will continue to shape our academic programs with respect for the diversity of our students and our community. We encourage interdisciplinary learning and seek to prepare our students for the ever-changing, diverse world in which we live. In addition, our Extension Learning Program, open to all those with a high school diploma, encourages lifelong learning for the residents of Bleeker County.

There often is much confusion about the difference between a Vision Statement and a Mission Statement. Usually, a Vision Statement expresses what an organization stands for, while the Mission Statement clearly describes the "business" of the organization – what the organization does – or expresses the purpose for which the organization exists.

The following example from a community nature center helps to clarify the difference:

> *Vision: "A healthy environment sustainable for humans and all other life forms."*
> *Mission: "To educate about the natural world, and instill a compassion for all living things and to teach about ecological systems and conservation methods."*

While both the Vision Statement (if any) and the Mission Statement of the NPO are constant (unless revised or rewritten at some point by the Board of Directors), each program or project undertaken by the organization will have its own goals and objectives, consistent with the organization's mission.

A **Goal** is a broad-based statement of the ultimate result
of the change being undertaken.

There are no descriptions of *how* the NPO is going to accomplish the goal in the goal statement, just as a good mission statement for the organization does not state *how* the organization will accomplish its mission.

Here are three examples of goals:

> *Encourage women to take responsibility for their own financial well-being and self sufficiency. (Womankind's Financial Literacy Project)*

> *Entering freshman will be better prepared to learn and to participate in college life. (Bleeker College Fresh Start Program)*

> *The homebound elderly in Shangri-La County will live with dignity and independence in their own homes. (Shangri-La Senior Service Center)*

As you can see, these goals do not include *how* the goal is going to be met, unlike objectives, which do.

An **Objective** is a measurable, time-specific result that the organization expects to accomplish.

Objectives are much more narrowly defined than goals, and should show some sort of movement as a result of your activities. An objective can be stated as "who" will do "what" by "when." You may have several objectives to address each of your goals. Using the first goal just cited, here are four potential relevant objectives:

> *Goal: Encourage women to take responsibility for their own financial well-being and self sufficiency. (Womankind's Financial Literacy Project)*

> *Objective 1: With input from financial professionals, members, and the Board, Womankind staff will create the curriculum for a six-week, introductory Financial Literacy course by January 1, 2011.*

> *Objective 2: The Training Coordinator will train at least two new Financial Literacy Course Facilitators by February 15, 2011.*

Objective 3: Womankind instructors will offer the first Financial Literacy Course for 20 women, beginning April, 2011.

Objective 4: The Executive Director will fill all six 2011 classes by December 31.

To clarify:

- Goals are lofty intentions; objectives are exact.
- Goals are intangible; objectives are tangible.
- Goals are broad; objectives are focused.
- Goals cannot be measured; objectives can be measured.

Well-conceived and well-written goals and objectives should:

- Tie directly to the case statement.
- Include all relevant parties in the target population.
- Allow plenty of time to accomplish the objectives, and
- Be specific enough that they can be measured (evaluated).

If there is no way to measure change, you are either describing a goal, or you will need to rethink the objective you are trying to state. Objectives do not describe methods and the many tasks by which you are going to accomplish the objective. They should describe a result.

In the example above, evidence that the first objective was accomplished would be the written curriculum documents. Evidence that the second objective was met could include a test taken by the new facilitators showing that they learned the training materials.

There are several different ways to categorize objectives. In human services, for example, objectives often measure knowledge (changes in learning or skills), attitude (changes in opinion and approach) and behavior (changes in ability or performance).

Good objectives begin with good verbs. What verbs did you have in the very first sentence you wrote ("what is the purpose of your project?")? Can your verb be found on the following list?

To act as	To enhance	To offer
To address	To enlighten	To orchestrate
To advance	To ensure	To organize
To aim	To estimate	To plan
To alleviate	To examine	To predict
To allow	To expand	To preserve
To ameliorate	To fill	To prevent
To analyze	To fix	To provide
To apply	To foster	To promote
To articulate	To gather	To question
To ascertain	To guarantee	To reduce
To assess	To generate	To relieve
To assist	To grow	To reproduce
To assure	To heal	To review
To better	To help	To revitalize
To bring	To impart	To save
To build	To implement	To secure
To calculate	To increase	To select
To celebrate	To inspire	To serve
To collaborate	To integrate	To share
To compose	To interpret	To solve
To contribute	To interview	To stop
To create	To learn	To strive
To define	To manifest	To support
To determine	To measure	To sustain
To develop	To motivate	To target
To discover	To nourish	To teach
To educate	To observe	To train
To encourage	To obtain	To transform

A **Logic Model** is a representation in graph form of how a program or project
uses its resources to create activities which have measurable results
that lead to desired outcomes.

Not only is a Logic Model useful in determining how to evaluate your project or program (see Lesson Six), but it can help you think clearly about end results as you design your program. The "activities/results/outcomes" language used in a logic model often is interchangeable with "action steps/objectives/goals" used elsewhere in this *Guide*.

Inputs are resources to be used
in your program.

Examples of inputs are: agency staff, agency space and equipment, collaborating agency services, and/or foundation grant and other funds dedicated to the proposed program or project. These can include resources already in place, resources to be purchased with the grant funds, or matching and in-kind services. For instance, a housing rehabilitation program may have five professional staff members supervising thirty-five volunteers, to make a dilapidated building available to a low-income family. Inputs would be: the building, the tools, the materials, the staff, and the labor of the volunteers.

Activities are specific actions to be done
with the inputs.

Some examples of activities are:

- *In preparation for the Fresh Start orientation week, the Office of Health Services Director will brief staff and administrators on its program.*

- *The staff and Director will create and review a curriculum for its workshop.*
- *The staff will produce individual curriculum packets for all participants.*
- *During the Fresh Start week, the Office of Health Services will conduct a workshop for all freshman students on STD prevention.*
- *Before and after the workshop, students will be given a brief test of their knowledge, attitude, and behaviors with respect to STD prevention.*

Outputs are tangible or measurable products of your proposal's or project's activities.

Outputs may be tangible, such as an educational video tape, a new homeless shelter building, or food distributed at a community food pantry. Or they may be measurable, such as the number of students who passed a test, the number of children sheltered in foster homes, or the miles of roadway cleaned up.

For the example objective:

> *"Two hundred Bleeker freshmen will be educated on the threat of STDs and how to prevent infection."*

The outputs could include:

- *Attractive, student-designed posters promoting good health habits, posted in dormitories and other campus buildings.*
- *A detailed packet of safe sex information assembled by staff to distribute at the Fresh Start workshop, and available on the college's website.*
- *Text messages sent every Friday afternoon reminding freshmen to have a nice weekend and, if they are sexually active, to practice safe sex.*

The **Outcome** is the change or changes that will occur

as a result of your proposal's outputs.

In other words, the outcome is the impact of your program on the problem that you are attempting to address. It is a demonstrable change from the conditions that existed prior to your activities. For example:

Bleeker College students are less likely to become infected with STDs.

Measurement is the instrument by which outcomes are calculated or described.

Data methods can be either quantitative, that is, described in numerical terms, or qualitative, describe in narrative terms, or both.

Quantitative Measurement: The Bleeker Health Services Department and the Bleeker County Public Health Office will measure the number of new reported cases of STDs, and will compare this number to last year's.

Qualitative Measurement: In an annual survey conducted by the Health Services Department, Bleeker students will self-report safer sex measures, such as condom usage, abstinence, and discussions with partners.

▶ **Exercise:**

Write or review the goals and objectives for your program or project. Do they meet the criteria defined here? Are they short, clear, and to the point? Are the objectives specific and measurable? If yes, proceed. If not, keep revising the goals and objectives until they meet the definitions provided here.

Matching the project to the participants

Next, you will define for whom your program is intended. In other words, who will be served? In a few paragraphs or a short list, explain who you will attempt to reach, serve, or help. How will you find them or how will they find you? How will they be selected? How will they be recruited? Many activities to recruit participants also are opportunities to market your project. Here is an example:

In addition to the ongoing classes, we plan to:

- *Expand the number of six-week Core Courses offered in Greater Boston from three to six, each serving up to twenty women.*
- *Add one class series each in Groton, Concord, and one other location to be determined.*
- *Add one class series specifically designed for the needs of the women in the large Greater Boston Brazilian community, to be taught in Portuguese.*

In order to reach these women and fill these classes, activities include:

- *Design and distribute flyers at libraries, women's groups, houses of worship, nursery schools, and senior centers.*
- *Send emails to all alumnae, inviting them to tell friends about the classes.*
- *Submit articles to local newspapers featuring interviews with recent course graduates, as well as announcements to community news websites.*
- *Develop new courses, which will generate news articles in local media.*
- *Offer on-site lectures and workshops for area women's organizations, including the 45-minute interactive workshop "Introduction to Financial Literacy for Women."*
- *Make tuition assistance available to help low-moderate income women.*
- *Offer both online and mail-in registration options.*

► **Exercise:**

In a few paragraphs, explain for whom this project is intended, how they will be selected or recruited, and how they will find you.

Constructing a logic model

The next task is to describe in detail how you propose to implement your project. What exactly do you plan to do? What outcomes do you anticipate? In terms of managing and supporting personnel, space requirements, equipment, materials, and supplies, what is needed to accomplish the project and its outcomes? What preliminary ideas do you have about how the success of the project will be measured? One way to help organize this information and your project is to construct a Logic Model.

Financial Literacy Project

INPUTS	ACTIVITIES	OUTPUTS	OUTCOMES	MEASUREMENT
Resources to be used by the project.	*What the project will do with the inputs provided.*	*Products of the project.*	*Changes that will occur as a result of the outputs.*	*Instrument used to measure outcomes.*
❖ Volunteer instructors ❖ Agency classroom space ❖ Marketing brochures ❖ FLP Workbook ❖ Big Bucks Foundation grant ❖ Participant tuition fees	❖ Create 6-week Curriculum ❖ Train additional facilitators to accommodate demand ❖ Run new FLP course for 20 women by Spring 2010 ❖ Run six FLP classes during 2010, for up to 20 per class	❖ 60-120 women will attend 6-week course in basic money management ❖ Two or more women will be trained as FLP facilitators	❖ At least 90% of attendees will feel more confident about their money ❖ 90% of attendees will be responsible for their own financial well-being and self-sufficiency	❖ Pre- and post-evaluation survey to measure feelings about managing money, and changes made in money handling ❖ Number of attendees at each class

▶ **Exercise:**

Using the example given, construct a Logic Model for your project.

Creating a project timeline

Once you have listed all your goals (or desired outcomes) and objectives (or activities), and have thought through the specific action steps needed to meet those objectives, as well as how long it will take to accomplish them, then you can create a timeline for your project. You can do so as a simple table in a word processing program or set up a spreadsheet. Keep the timetable to one page by listing only the major milestones, not every minor sub-task. If you are unsure when the program or project will begin, use generic headers such as Month 1, Month 2 or Quarter 1, Quarter 2. Do be realistic and allow ample time for each task, including some time for unforeseen contingencies!

► **Exercise:**

Using the example provided below as a model, construct a timeline for your project.

Sample Project Timeline: Financial Literacy Project

Activities	Month	Nov			Dec		Jan			Feb			Mar			Apr		May		
Task	**Day**	17					4	15		15			10			8		14	21	
Hold meeting to gather input for Financial Literacy Curriculum		█																		
Staff creates new FL Curriculum for 6-week introductory course						█														
New Curriculum printed									█											
Develop training program for Course Facilitators									█											
Recruit new course facilitators					█	█														
Train at least 2 new course Facilitators										█										
Develop Marketing Plan for new course:										█										
- Online registration										█	█									
- Mail, P.R.											█									
Market, Promote course												█	█	█	█					
Course Registration opens													█							
First Course Begins																█				
Course ends, distribute evaluation materials & collect it																		█		
Analyze course evaluations																		█	█	
Summarize evaluations, report results to funders																				█

▶ **Exercise:**

Review the considerable work you have accomplished in this Lesson. Be sure that you have described clearly what you plan to do, for whom the project is intended, the activities you will undertake, and the resources needed to accomplish your objectives. Be certain that the timeline is realistic, and that one activity builds upon the next to a logical goal. Make any necessary changes or additions.

As you do this review, you may find that your organization does not have all the resources needed to complete the project. Or you may find that obtaining all the needed resources would drain the organization's capacity to do other important work. If this is so, you may want to consider a collaboration with one or more other organizations with similar missions. To learn more, go to **Lesson Five**.

Lesson Five: Consider a Collaboration

Collaboration – that is, two or more organizations working together on the same project – is increasingly popular in the world of grant funding. Especially in a challenging economic climate, funders recognize that drawing on the strength, talent, expertise, and resources of more than one organization can be a recipe for success. Of course, there also can be pitfalls. As you develop your project, here are some relevant factors to consider as you make the decision as to whether collaboration is right for your organization.

- Have you clearly identified the need?
- What is necessary to address that need?
- If you don't have all the tools, skills, personnel, space and other resources – who does?
- Can you hire someone, contract for, or obtain the needed resources?
- Will collaboration enhance your ability to serve your constituents?
- Should you choose to work with a similar or a complementary organization?
- Are there some good potential partners whom you can trust?
- Who should your partner(s) be?

Types of collaborations

There are three main kinds of collaborations:

1. Two or more NPOs with similar missions, but different constituents. For example:

   *The Organization for the Moon River collaborated with Halcyon Valley Trustees,
   and the Wild and Scenic River Council, to:*

   - *Co-sponsor annual events.*
   - *Apply for funding.*
   - *Respond to a regulatory or legislative matter.*
   - *Co-sponsor a long-term study.*

- *Conduct a watershed roundtable every two years of all the small river, stream, lake, and pond groups in the Moon, Halcyon, and Wild and Scenic watersheds to disseminate information, and to offer guidance and technical expertise to one another.*
- *Share staff (only one of the NPOs has a professional scientist on staff who monitors water quality).*
- *Bring together staff and volunteers, who may feel isolated, to give a good snapshot of what others are doing, along with an opportunity to articulate their needs.*

2. Two or more NPOs with different missions that overlap. For example:

The Bleeker County Foundation for Better Hearing offers education and screening and "provides advocacy, support, and resources for those with hearing disorders." Since hearing loss is an occupational hazard in certain professions, this organization might collaborate with the local chapter of a pilots' association or an organization of professional rock musicians on prevention education.

3. A non-profit focused on a particular cause can team up with a for-profit company that is known for its support of that cause. For example:

Avon and breast cancer, Verizon Wireless and domestic violence prevention organizations, Whole Foods and sustainable agriculture and food pantries.

Guidelines for successful collaborations

Collaborations often form for a short-term, time-limited project, but could develop into a longer-term, strategic working relationship. For successful collaborations:

- Know your NPO's core values. Select partners with compatible values, missions, or philosophies. Trust is essential at the outset.

- Discuss expectations at the start. What does each party want? One partner might want to raise money, another to get new members, publicity, or to sponsor a fun activity for members. For example, if each party wants a collaborative project to look different and each has different goals, they are likely to disagree about whether it was a success.

- Discuss and agree on details:
    a. What resources will each partner contribute?
    b. How will grants or earned income be distributed? The split should be fair, and in proportion to what each organization is contributing.
    c. Who will do exactly what work?
    d. How much (if any) will they be paid?
    e. Who is in charge of coordination, and for keeping things moving along?
    f. How will the credit be shared publicly?
    g. Who will do the publicity? Who is the media spokesperson?
    h. What are the deliverables?
    i. When are they due?
    j. Who will own any intellectual property produced?
    k. How will success be measured?

- Determine whether the organizations will continue to collaborate, or if this is a one-time effort. You also will need to discuss how to make this decision. For example, consider what would happen if one of the parties thinks the project was a resounding success and wants to continue on a permanent basis, while the other party does not want a long-term commitment.

If you do decide to collaborate, you should prepare a document, such as a Memorandum of Understanding, so that each organization has a clear understanding of the partnership. All parties will contribute to developing the project and writing the proposals. All parties should review the final agreement and the Board President or Executive Director of each organization should sign it.

▶   **Exercise:**

Identify at least two potential collaborators for your project, and list the reasons for choosing them. What does each bring to the table? What might be the possible challenges or difficulties in working together? Proceed to **Lesson Six**.

Lesson Six: Evaluate Your Project

A non-profit organization holds a special tax-exempt designation, because it serves the public trust. Every time your agency asks for and receives funding, it has an obligation to ensure that its programs create, and will continue to create, the desired results. If they do not, it is the agency's obligation to explain why.

In addition, good evaluation results will help to further knowledge in your field. Perhaps your assumptions about a certain population or problem were incorrect, and you can prevent other NPOs from making the same error. Evaluation is the tool you will use to meet this obligation.

Clearly defined and articulated goals and objectives[1] will describe the results of implementing your program. In other words, if the funder gives you the requested funds, and you complete the project, what will the future situation look like?

In order to demonstrate the measurability of your project or program's effectiveness, it is critical to design the evaluation component as you write the proposal. Funders frequently require that the evaluation component be incorporated into a proposal. Even if this information is not specifically requested, it is a good idea to show the funder that your organization has determined how the project or program will be evaluated, prior to implementation. It just might give your proposal a competitive edge!

There are several questions to be considered as you create your evaluation design. They include: How do you plan to evaluate your project? What qualitative and/or quantitative methods will be used? Who will develop them, and what resources are needed to do so? How much of your budget will be spent on evaluation? Who will conduct the evaluation, and how will the evaluative process be implemented? How and by whom will the data collected be analyzed? How will you disseminate the results of the analysis?

---

[1] Or outcomes and activities, using Logic Model language.

As illustrated in the diagram below, evaluation measures are derived from the program objectives, which are determined by the program goals, which in turn are derived from the community need the program is designed to serve.

Using your program objectives, the evaluation will determine whether they were met, partially met, or unmet.

- *We will serve 250 teens in our after-school program this year, a 25% increase from last year.* (How many actually were served?)

- *Each weekday, we feed an average of 32 seniors a nutritious lunch, but with [amount] more funding, we could serve 50.* (How many were fed?)

- *The number of cases of sexually-transmitted diseases reported to the Bleeker College Campus Health Services office will decrease by 20% during Year One, and by 40% by the end of Year Two.* (Percentage of STD case decrease?)

Types of evaluation measures

Using the example of the Financial Literacy Project, evaluation could consist of quantitative methods, such as:

At least nineteen women will successfully complete the first six-week course.

This number could be documented by tabulating the results of a post-test given to the students, or simply by taking attendance at each of the six classes.

Or the methods could be qualitative, such as quotes or anecdotes from clients or program participants. These narratives can be very effective illustrators of your agency's or program's success. Don't be afraid to use a qualitative method to show that your program is on the right track, accomplishing what you have intended. For example:

> *"I knew very little about our family finances before taking the FLP course. Now I am much more confident, and I'm reorganizing my retirement portfolio!" – Mary Ann P., age 61*
>
> *"After my divorce, I felt frightened about my financial situation. I couldn't make ends meet, and worried about my children's future. My friend recommended your FLP course, and even though I didn't have much money, I knew I had to take it, to help myself and to keep my kids from ending up terrified like me. Now I have a good job, have eliminated my debt, and I am saving for our future!" – Kim B., age 36*

Additionally, an evaluation can be either "formative" or "summative." *Formative* evaluation provides information during the course of the project or program, so that any necessary changes or improvements can be made along the way. A mid-term exam is a good example of a formative evaluation. Inviting a panel of experts to review a staff-developed curriculum before it is implemented is another example of formative evaluation.

Summative evaluation shows the effectiveness of the program or project at its conclusion or even at some future point in time. It describes goals met and objectives obtained, either fully or in part.

The challenge of evaluation

Historically, human services, education, and the arts – organizations which seek to improve the quality of life – have been the most difficult to evaluate. For example, it is virtually impossible to say that an adult registering to vote does so because of the encouragement and instruction he or she received in a 6th grade civics class or after-school club. The results of that class or club simply cannot be measured, as there are too many other contributing factors. And while performing arts organizations can collect anecdotal evidence via exit surveys or interviews about how an audience enjoyed a performance, it would not be easy to actually measure improvement in the quality of life of one particular audience member.

In order to improve the effectiveness of evaluation, a growing trend in recent years has been Outcome Measurement.

What is Outcome Measurement?

Funders, the government, and taxpayers increasingly are looking for more evidence that the money they are providing or the donations they make are having the intended impact on peoples' lives. And those who work in and volunteer for NPOs are eager to know that their work makes a difference. Thus, logic models, with their clear outcomes delineated, are becoming more commonly used for human service organizations.

In short, Outcome Measurement is about accountability: "Is this program or service really making a difference?" According to the United Way, an outcome measurement is: "A regular systematic method of tracking the extent to which those who participate in your programs experience intended benefits or changes."[2] The United Way website also provides a good introduction to Outcome Measurement for those who wish to learn more.

Depending on the size of the grant for which you are applying, you might plan to spend anywhere from 3% to 10% of your total budget on evaluation. If the program is complex, organizations can outsource the evaluation design and analysis for their programs. Having an outside evaluation is also a good way to avoid the bias inherent in self-evaluation. To find consultants who specialize in evaluation, you can contact your local United Way, community foundation, or grantmaker library for recommendations.

---

[2] http://www.liveunited.org/outcomes/.

▶ **Exercises:**

Using the goals and objectives you created in **Lesson Five**, briefly describe how you plan to evaluate your program or project. Who will develop, implement, and analyze the evaluation measure(s), and how will the results be used or disseminated? How will you know if/when the project or program is succeeding or is successful? Another way to address this question is: What will a successful program/project outcome look like?

Now that you have thought through and carefully described the evaluation process, you can begin to create a budget for your project in **Lesson Seven.**

Lesson Seven: Create Your Project Budget

Once you have completed all the previous steps, you can create a budget. Start by listing or estimating costs for the personnel, materials, equipment, and space you described in your methods section, as well as other direct costs needed for your project. Then, list how you will bring in money (revenues) and determine whether you have an excess of revenue or a deficit. As you begin to create your budget, consider:

- How important is this project to your agency? Is it important enough to dedicate agency dollars beyond the requested grant?
- Is it important enough to forgo administrative costs and put all the requested money into services?
- Can you build administrative costs proportionally into the budget?
- Can you leverage your contributions (in-kind or otherwise)? (Government granting agencies in particular like to see this matching of contributions.)
- If this is a reimbursement grant (again, often the case with government agencies) can you carry the project or program until reimbursement arrives?

Your budget must show that the revenue you seek from this funder, plus the revenue you are likely to be able to raise, or already have raised elsewhere, will pay for the program or project. For example, if the total needed for your project is $300,000, and you are requesting $20,000 from this funder, you must be able to convince the funder that you have a realistic plan to secure the remaining $280,000. Most funders will ask you to list other supporters and the amounts they have pledged as well as other foundations and agencies to which you intend to apply. It is highly unlikely that a funder would make a grant to an organization which is unrealistically optimistic about projected income. The rare exception is the case of a brand-new organization applying for start-up funds (a "seed" grant).

The balance of needed funds can come from the organization's operating budget, from charging a fee for program services, or from other development efforts. You may want to refer back to the diagram in Lesson One, "Revenue Components," which lists the most common sources of NPO revenues, as you create your budget.

If the funder does not provide a budget form, you may be able to obtain a budget template form at your local grantmaking library, or you can adapt the one below. Your bookkeeper, treasurer, business manager, or financial officer will need to track income and expenses for the project once funding is received, so now is a good time to consult with them about the expense categories they use. You may need to rework categories from your agency's line items to conform to the funder's budget templates. We recommend updating your organizational budget yearly on a state or national budget template, so that you are always ready when grant deadlines approach. Here is a sample budget:

PROJECT NAME: Financial Literacy Project
Funder Name: Big Bucks Foundation
Fiscal Year End: 6/30/09

	Project Budget		Organizational Budget
	This Request	Total Project Budget	Total Organization Budget
Income Sources			
Government Grants			
Foundation and Corporate Grants	5,000	7,500	30,000
United Way			
Individual Contributions			37,891
Earned Income		1,710	10,000
Interest Income			
In-Kind Support			8,750
Other Income			18,680
Total Income	**5,000**	**9,210**	**105,321**
Expenses			
Salaries and Wages	4,000	5,500	40,400
Employee Benefits and Taxes @ 28%		560	11,312
Total Personnel Costs	**4,000**	**6,060**	**51,712**
Bank/Investment Fees			100
Equipment Rental & Maintenance			4,165
Food Costs	48	100	250
Fundraising/Development Expenses			21,240
Insurance Expense			1,520
Marketing/Advertising		890	1,050
Postage and Delivery	252	500	940
Professional Development			750
Professional Fees			8,750
Rent and Occupancy		780	6,240
Supplies and Materials	700	700	950
Telephone Expense		113	900
Travel Expense		07	500
Dues & Subscriptions			2,154
Consultant Expense			4,000
Miscellaneous Expenses			100
Total Non Personnel Costs	**1,000**	**3,150**	**53,609**
Total Expenses	**5,000**	**9,210**	**105,321**
Excess of Revenue Over Expenses	-	**0**	-

Budget Narrative:
INCOME:
In-Kind support represents time of Ex. Director to oversee program at 1% of salary.
Earned Income = tuition paid by 19 class attendees, $90/per person

EXPENSES:
Salaries for the project include Ex. Director time for curriculum and staff oversight ($1500) &
    a training coordinator for 4 hours per week @ $25/hr for 40 weeks.
Postage to mail new class announcement to mailing list at $.44
Food = partial refreshments for course attendees.
Travel = course lecturers mileage reimbursement. @$.48/mile
Supplies/Materials = Printing new course curriculum for class participants during 2010.
Marketing/Advertising = Printed materials (e.g. flyers, ads)

ORGANIZATION BUDGET NOTES:
Other Income represents annual raffle proceeds ($8,000) and special event (silent auction).
Salary represents part-time Executive Director (.5 FTE) @ $35 / hr. and training coordinator (.1 FTE) @ $25/hr.

Copyright 2009
Carla C. Cataldo Gail R. Shapiro

Writing a budget narrative

Note that the budget expenses and revenues should balance. In some cases, a small revenue excess may be appropriate, but a deficit rarely will be viewed positively by the funder. In-kind services or agency surpluses from prior years (the Fund Balance) can help balance a budget as well.

Make sure to explain anything unusual or counter-intuitive in your budget in the budget narrative, and to provide as much detail as possible. In particular, note any consultants you plan to use, their qualifications, and how they were selected. If this is a capital project, note how many estimates were obtained so that the funder knows you are using a realistic price and have worked to contain costs via a competitive bid process.

Instead of listing a staff person's annual salary, you can express the expense as an hourly or weekly rate, and the number of hours per week that the employee will dedicate to the project or program for which you are requesting funds. Here are some ways to express expenses for salaries:

Staff position	Salary	Time	Request
Director	$100,000	10%	$10,000
Social worker	$ 50/hr	3 hr/wk, 24 wks	$ 3,600
Clerical support	$ 45,000	.2 FTE[3]	$ 9,000
Youth educator	$ 32,000	100%	$32,000

Not only will listing the staff positions this way serve as a good math check for you, it will answer questions ahead of time for the funder, such as whether the position is full- or part-time. It is better to offer the information, rather than have the funder guess, be unclear, or assume incorrectly. Also, be sure to state how your agency defines a full-time week (e.g. 40, 37.5, or 35 hours).

The question of how to value in-kind labor often arises. As a rule, if a professional is providing his or her professional skills for the project, you can value them at the customary rate. If the volunteer is an attorney who normally charges $250/hour, but in this program she is helping to paint the

---

[3] Full-Time Equivalent.

homeless shelter, her time must be valued at the going rate for painters, not at the customary rate for legal counsel.

In this section of the proposal, most funders also will want to see or hear about your future funding strategies, once the grant period ends. They do not want to help create a new program that will dissolve in following years because they and your agency no longer can fund it. Include some information or ideas on where future dollars will come from. Just stating that you will seek future funding is not good enough! The more specific you can be, the better.

Some examples for future funding include: applying for government funding, once the pilot program has been evaluated successfully; dedicating a larger percentage of agency funds to the project; increasing development efforts by hiring more staff or consultants; or creating a revenue stream from the proposed program, such as via user fees, tuition, or ticket sales.

▶ **Exercise:**

Using the template provided here, create a budget and a budget narrative for your program or project, taking care to explain any unusual line items. Then go on to **Lesson Eight** to learn how to customize and submit your proposal.

PROJECT NAME:

Funder Name: **Fiscal Year End:**

	Project Budget			Organizational Budget
	This Request	**Total Project Budget**		**Total Organization Budget**
Income Sources				
Government Grants				
Foundation and Corporate Grants				
United Way				
Individual Contributions				
Earned Income				
Interest Income				
In-Kind Support				
Other Income				
Total Income				
Expenses				
Salaries and Wages				
Employee Benefits and Taxes @ %				
Total Personnel Costs				
Bank/Investment Fees				
Equipment Rental & Maintenance				
Food Costs				
Fundraising/Development Expenses				
Insurance Expense				
Marketing/Advertising				
Postage and Delivery				
Professional Development				
Professional Fees				
Rent and Occupancy				
Supplies and Materials				
Telephone Expense				
Travel Expense				
Dues & Subscriptions				
Consultant Expense				
Miscellaneous Expenses				
Total Non Personnel Costs				
Total Expenses				
Excess of Revenue Over Expenses				

Budget Narrative:

INCOME:

EXPENSES:

Lesson Eight: Customize and Submit Your Proposal

Now that you have developed a good proposal, you want to send it to all your possible good funder matches, to increase your chances of success. How do you send out a single proposal to multiple funders? By tailoring it to meet the goals and requirements of each funder. Below are two excerpts from proposals sent to two different funders for the same project. What can you tell about the funders from these excerpts? What types of funders are they likely to be? In other words, who is the audience the writer is addressing?

Excerpt #1:

We believe that Womankind's mission to promote economic self-sufficiency for the women of Massachusetts is consistent with the priority of the ABC Corporate Contributions Program to promote the quality of opportunities for women, and to support new and collaborative approaches to addressing problems. The Financial Literacy Project, targeted especially at women and children at risk for poverty, depends upon its constituents, not only for the actual planning and testing of the program, but also for teaching on a woman-to-woman basis. By submitting companion proposals to family, community, and corporate foundations, and by encouraging local businesses and organizations to participate, we expect this project to become a collaborative effort of the entire community, and to be fully self-sustaining after Year Three.

Excerpt #2:

Operating support in the amount of $10,000 from the XYZ FOUNDATION will enable Womankind to implement the Financial Literacy Project (FLP), and ensure that the program is accessible to the following populations: girls, long-living women, women who are differently-abled, women of color, lesbians, low-income women, women in transition, and immigrant women. Topics in the collaboratively-written handbook will include: economic inequality, opening a bank account, financing a home, responsible investing, and the growing awareness of the collective power of women's philanthropy. Through the FLP, Womankind will continue to serve the needs of women, including those of us who are the most vulnerable and have the least access to resources.

Can you tell the difference? If you are not sure, go back and re-read the **Sources of foundation funding** section in Lesson Two before reading ahead.

The first excerpt was from a proposal sent to a bank, while the second was sent to a local women's foundation. Even though the project is exactly the same, for each proposal, the writer chose to highlight the aspects of the project that were most closely aligned with the mission and purpose – and yes, the politics – of the funder. This technique is known as "tailoring a proposal" to the audience. The outcome in this case? Both proposals were funded.

Sometimes, it is difficult to tell from published guidelines how appropriate a match a particular funder may be for your project. That is one reason many more foundations and some corporate contribution officers are encouraging letters of inquiry, calls, or emails prior to submittals. You can use this opportunity to determine the appropriateness of the funding match, geographic priority, and so on. This call is especially important if the guidelines are very broad, or are not completely clear. Often, a computer database search will pick up lots of potential funders, but these are not always good matches for your project or organization.

For example, depending on the funder, the term "Greater Boston" may mean the City of Boston only; or Boston, plus the neighboring cities of Cambridge, Somerville, and Chelsea; or anywhere inside Route 128, which circles Boston and its suburbs; or all of Eastern Massachusetts! Don't guess. It is fine to call or email the funder for clarification.

Although email may seem easier or more cost effective, the information you can obtain from a phone conversation will prove its worth. For example, you may be able to gauge your proposal's likely chances from the funder's responses, or determine that it is not worth the time to apply since most of a funder's assets may be set aside for other long-term funding commitments.

You must resist the temptation to submit the exact same proposal to multiple funders. Always look at your template proposal after reviewing a specific funder's guidelines, and take the time to tailor your response, so that your proposal will stand out. More importantly, you will avoid the potential for embarrassing error. Unfortunately, funders sometimes receive proposals addressed to another funder, or proposals that clearly do not match their published guidelines. Avoiding these obvious mistakes will improve your chances for success and will help preserve your agency's professional reputation.

Addenda

Unless otherwise specified, any addenda requested by the funder should follow the budget page, with the exception of the cover letter, which is placed at the top of the proposal packet. If the funder has not specified what should be attached (and has *not* specifically directed that nothing be attached), include the following:

- IRS determination letter of 501(c)(3) status.
- Current operating budget of the organization (in addition to the project budget) and audited financial statement.
- List of the Board of Directors and their affiliations.
- Letter(s) of support, from the collaborator(s), if any, or from a government official, such as your state representative or mayor.

The cover letter

Submitted with each proposal is a cover letter, which briefly introduces the organization, the project, and states the request for funding. It should be one page, written on organization letterhead, and signed by the organization's most senior officer, normally the Executive Director or Board President. Here is a sample format:

DATE
Salutation

On behalf of the Board of Directors of NAME OF YOUR ORGANIZATION, I am pleased to present this request for DOLLAR AMOUNT to the NAME OF FOUNDATION/COMPANY.

This request will: (PROJECT SUMMARY HERE).

VERY brief description of organization with agency's mission:

Mention of any past funding, with thanks. End with positive statement, such as: "We look forward to working with NAME OF FOUNDATION to help (address the problem you will describe in proposal.)" I am happy to answer any questions. Thank you for your consideration of this request.

Sincerely yours,
ORGANIZATION PRESIDENT or EXECUTIVE DIRECTOR

Packaging and delivering your proposal

Once you have written the cover letter, thoroughly proofread the proposal, double-checked the math in the budget, and reviewed the funder's guidelines, you are ready to package and deliver your proposal.

Many funders require proposals to be submitted electronically, either as an email attachment, or more frequently, via a form on its website. The latter may require a frustrating exercise of "cut-and-paste," and you will be limited to a specific number of characters per section. Also, you may not be allowed to use underlines, footnotes, or other "non-standard" formatting.

For proposals submitted via mail, you may be asked specifically not to use expensive papers, fancy bindings, or costly covers. Again, be sure to follow the funder's guidelines for format, font size, number of copies, and any specific instructions for submitting the proposal. This is especially critical when the funder expects to receive a very large number of proposals, such as is often the case for government grants. Do not give the funder an excuse to disqualify your proposal. Making a mistake seemingly as simple as stapling the proposal when the instructions say to submit it without fasteners can land your hours of hard work in the trash!

Be sure your proposal is ready well ahead of the funder's stated deadline, if there is one. A late proposal will be rejected automatically. Some funders will specify that you use standard US Mail rather than costly overnight express delivery. Many funders use the postmark date on the envelope as evidence that you met the deadline. Government agencies are particularly sensitive to the time stamp. Hand delivery may be appropriate if you know the funder personally.

The letter of inquiry or concept paper

Funders sometimes ask for a "Letter of Inquiry" (LOI) or a "Concept Paper," which presents a brief description of your project, instead of a full proposal. If the funder is interested in the project, they then will invite you to submit a full proposal. If after reviewing your LOI they are not interested, most often they will not contact you at all.

Unless otherwise directed by the funder, the Letter of Inquiry should be one page, briefly identifying your agency, your requested amount, the request and why it is needed, and what the expected outcome will be.

A Concept Paper normally is three to five pages, maximum. Instead of a one-sentence description of the topics included in a Letter of Inquiry, you can flesh out each sentence into a full paragraph, and add more information about why the agency should implement the idea, any potential or planned collaborations, and some information about the intended evaluation. And be sure to express your desire to submit a full proposal.

Dos and don'ts

We have walked you through the entire process of writing a classic grant proposal. Have you been doing the exercises? If so, your proposal is just about ready to go. Below are some important tips for proposal writing, based on our combined 55 years of experience, both as proposal writers and as reviewers, as well as some advice on following up whether you get the grant or get a rejection letter.

Do:
- Cultivate a relationship with your funder through preliminary contact, such as a phone call or email, rather than sending in a blind proposal.
- Carefully follow all rules and guidelines, and adhere to deadlines.
- Use the funder's language if possible. However, do not use incorrect terminology. If you find language that is different from the definitions we have provided, do ask the funder to clarify what it is they seek. You even may help to educate their staff and/or Board.
- Be clear, concise, and compelling!

- Send an email or call to confirm that your letter or proposal was received, unless the guidelines specify otherwise.

- Be responsive if more information or a site visit is required.

- Use a Letter of Inquiry or Concept Paper before submitting a full proposal, if allowed.

- Be polite, respectful, and confident in your project.

- See the funder as a potential partner in your work and address them accordingly.

- Ask your Board of Directors if they have any connection to the funder. A letter from a business acquaintance or a mention during a game of golf can improve your organization's chance of funding. Relationships matter.

- Proofread your proposal carefully.

- Have someone who is not familiar with the grant request also proofread the proposal before you send it.

Don't:

- Annoy the funder with lots of phone calls or emails. Make sure you have all of your questions ready before you make contact.

- Be rude or presumptuous. For example, do not call the funder to describe an idea for a project in detail and ask them if they think this is good match. It is *your* job to do the research to determine a good match, and to have a good proposal idea ready before calling!

- Think the rules don't apply to you. If you submit your proposal with more pages than the funder specifies; staple the proposal when they have requested a loose binding; send an insufficient number of copies; or if your proposal is sloppy, full of typographical errors, or arrives late; it very well may be thrown into the trash, no matter how worthwhile your project.

- Send a full proposal when the funder has specified a Letter of Inquiry or a Concept Paper.

- Omit requested information, thinking they "won't miss it."

- Send in a proposal "over the transom," that is, unsolicited or without regard to the funder's guidelines or deadlines.

- Fail to pay attention to timing. Don't call program officers the day before their foundation's Board of Directors is due to meet!

What to do when you DON'T get the grant

If you don't get the grant, of course you will be disappointed – but there's always next year (or the next funding cycle)! Even though your request was rejected this time, you still are in a relationship with this funder. Think of it as an opportunity to reformulate the program or at least to fine-tune the proposal. Here are some tips:

- Unless the funder has otherwise specified, you can call for constructive feedback. You may get some useful information for the next time you apply to this funder.
- We suggest that you write a thank-you letter to the funder for having considered your proposal, ("...while naturally we are disappointed that you will not be able to fund our work, we appreciate the time you took to review our proposal..."). Although some large foundations discourage this practice, as it creates more paperwork for them, we think it is good manners and should always be done, unless the funder specifically requests otherwise. Sadly, our grantmaking colleagues report that in any given cycle, they receive only one or two thank-you notes for dozens of grants!
- Pout, rant, or rave all you want in-house, but *never* say anything negative about the funder or its process outside your immediate circle. You don't know who is listening, or what their connection to the funder might be!

What to do when you DO get the grant

Hooray! You got the grant! Here's what to do next:

- Write a thank-you letter, signed by the President and/or Executive Director. Promptly. Always.
- Unless specifically requested *not* to do so (some funders make anonymous grants), publicize the grant with the funder's name prominently mentioned in printed materials and media releases.
- Ask the grantmaker if they have a standard blurb they would like you to use when giving them credit in publications, and whether or not they want you to include their logo.
- Send out a special media release announcing the grant.

- Send a half-year status report to the funder with press articles on the funded program/agency (or use the funder's specific form/status report evaluation) stating your intent to re-apply, if applicable. Be sure to use real, current numbers, trends, and/or anecdotes in progress reports. Do this even if they do not require it.

- Mark your calendar for next year's application dates.

- Review and execute any contracts or other paper work that may be required by the funder.

- Unless this is an unrestricted general operating grant, set up a fund within your bookkeeping system to track the grant income and expenses.

▶ **Exercise:**

If you will be submitting a full proposal, write a cover letter. When you are finished, ask someone who is not familiar with your project to review and proofread the entire proposal for you. Make any necessary corrections.

Congratulations! You now have finished a proposal that is ready for submission. Read on to learn about the business of grant proposal writing.

Appendix: Explore the Business of Grant Proposal Writing

How do you get started as a professional proposal writer? Most of us began by volunteering to raise funds for a non-profit organization with which we already were involved. Others found grant proposal writing a natural off-shoot of their job, for example, as Executive Director or Program Manager at a NPO.

Still others started by answering an ad for a "grant writer." (Note: this term often is used incorrectly. The one who writes the proposal is a "grant proposal writer;" the one who gives the money writes the grant.) Many times, little or no compensation is offered. If you decide to start via this route, do be careful. Many of these ads looking for cheap labor are placed by small or start-up non-profit organizations asking for free help in proposal writing. You obviously can choose to volunteer your time, either to get more experience in learning how to write proposals, or because you love the mission of the organization.

But for those who dream of becoming a professional in the field, and charging appropriately, it's important to understand that grant proposal writing is *not* simply creative writing, as you have learned in these eight lessons. It takes training, as well as technical knowledge, both in non-profit management as well as in the "business" of your client's organization. In addition, it requires an intimate knowledge of all the funders in your particular geographic area, as well as each one's specific focus and priorities.

Most grant proposal writers are hired by non-profits, schools, and agencies. Many others are freelance consultants working for a regular group of clients or taking occasional assignments in response to ads. Beware of offers to pay you a percentage of monies raised! Working on a percentage basis (or small fee plus percentage) not only is *not* advantageous either to the client or the writer, but it also violates the Code of Ethics of the Association of Fundraising Professionals (www.afpnet.org), to which many of us belong. It is unlikely that a professional who cares about advancing philanthropy and donor-based fundraising would work on a commission basis. In addition to being unethical, it devalues your time and skills.

While some proposal writers charge by the project, most charge by the hour, as it is difficult to tell ahead of time how long it will take to prepare a proposal, particularly if one has not worked before with a particular client. Much depends on what the client already has prepared, how cooperative they are about getting information to the writer in a timely way, whether this proposal is a top priority for them, and so on.

Before you accept even a volunteer position as a proposal writer, be sure that the program or project for which the client is requesting funds is fully developed, has a feasible budget, and a good evaluation component. Developing this material is the duty of the program staff who will be implementing the project or program. Missing any one of these components means that, in addition to being a proposal writer, you will be expected to serve as: program developer, evaluation specialist, budget developer, hand-holder, and maybe even drill sergeant!

An experienced proposal writer normally has some knowledge of all these components and skills. If you are called upon to do more than write the proposal itself, make sure you are properly compensated.

If you don't have experience in these areas, then volunteering with a NPO may be a good place to start one's career. Joining your local Association of Fundraising Professionals chapter also is a great way to obtain professional training and meet potential mentors and clients.

Keep copies of all proposals you write, even those that are not successful. You can learn as much from failures as from successes. Keep a simple spreadsheet "scorecard" of your successful proposals. It will aid you as you meet with prospective new clients. It is helpful to keep a list of the unsuccessful proposals on another worksheet, so you can keep track of what each funder is not likely to fund in the future.

Always be mindful of your client's confidentiality and proprietary information – grants are competitive, and the agency most likely will not want their work shared with others.

While the field is competitive, there is always room for good people in any profession. If you are not directly involved in providing vital services to a specific population to help them improve or change their lives, or in making your community more livable or beautiful, or in protecting our environment and its citizens, then obtaining money for those who do this work is a great contribution to make to the world. We wish you well in your endeavors.

Carla C. Cataldo and Gail R. Shapiro

August, 2009

About the Authors

As a Charitable Giving Consultant, Gail Shapiro helps individuals, families, and small business owners match their charitable gifts with their goals. She offers grant proposal writing and strategic planning services to non-profit organizations, as well as writing and editing services for companies and individuals. A frequent and popular speaker at local, regional, and national conferences, Ms. Shapiro's work has been featured in *The Christian Science Monitor*, *Working Mother*, *More*, *The Boston Globe*, *Bank Investing Marketing*, and *The Catalogue for Philanthropy*, as well as several publications, blogs, and TV and radio shows.

Ms. Shapiro has received commendations for her work from Massachusetts Senators Kennedy and Kerry, and in 2002, was honored as a "Daily Point of Light" by President Bush for her many years of volunteer service to the community.

In 1993, Ms. Shapiro founded Womankind Educational and Resource Center, Inc., and served as its Executive Director until June 2007. She also is the co-creator of Womankind's Financial Literacy Project®, designed to develop and provide economic literacy training for women. She is the editor of and contributing author to the Project's handbook, *Money Order: The Money Management Guide for Women* (Simon & Schuster, 2001). Formerly project administrator of the Harvard School Health Education Project at the Harvard School of Public Health, she is the author or co-author of four other non-fiction books and numerous articles. A graduate of Framingham State College, she holds a Master's degree in Educational Administration, Planning, and Social Policy from Harvard University. Contact her at: www.gailshapiro.com.

Carla C. Cataldo brings many years of government experience on the federal, state, and local level to her development consulting business. She has written successful proposals in the areas of: education, health and human services, economic development, transportation enhancements, housing, historical preservation, and the arts.

As the Executive Director of the Downtown Partnership of Milford, Inc., she revitalized a fledgling non-profit dedicated to downtown revitalization. During her tenure, membership more than tripled, and she was instrumental in securing a successful $500,000 grant from state Community Development Block Grant funds.

As the managing partner of Cataldo & Shapiro Proposal Writing and Consultation, she obtained a range of clients from new not-for-profit organizations such as Web of Benefit and EARTH Limited to large institutions such as the Radcliffe Institute for Advanced Studies and Milford Regional Medical Center.

She served as a member of the MetroWest Community Health Care Foundation's Distribution Committee for six years. Her writing experience includes both newspaper and magazine articles, newsletters, and direct-mail appeals. Degrees include a Master of Public Policy degree from Harvard University's John F. Kennedy School of Government, and an A.B. degree from Smith College. She makes numerous presentations on proposal writing for statewide and national organizations. Contact her at: www.proposalsetc.com.

www.ingramcontent.com/pod-product-compliance
Lightning Source LLC
Chambersburg PA
CBHW081219170526
45165CB00009B/2871